Série d'Ecriture
No. 20

Caroline Dubois

You Are the
Business

translated from the French by Cole Swensen

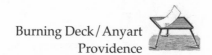

Burning Deck / Anyart
Providence

SERIE d'ECRITURE is an annual of current French writing in English translation. The first five issues were published by SPECTACULAR DISEASES, which continues to be a source for European distribution and subscription. Since No. 6, the publisher has been Burning Deck in Providence, RI.
Editor: Rosmarie Waldrop

Individual copies $14. Subscription for 2 issues: $24.
Supplements: $8, gratis to subscribers.

Distributors:
Small Press Distribution, 1341 Seventh St., Berkeley CA 94710
1-800/869-7553; orders@spdbooks.org
Spectacular Diseases, c/o Paul Green, 83b London Rd.,
Peterborough, Cambs. PE2 9BS
H Press, www.hpress.no
US subscriptions: Burning Deck, 71 Elmgrove Ave., Providence RI 02906

"talala" was first published in *The Germ 5 (2001)*.

Burning Deck Press is the Literature Program of ANYART: CONTEMPORARY ARTS CENTER, a tax-exempt (501c3), non-profit organization.

Cover by Keith Waldrop

contents

I wonder what the difference is between what you catch and what you create and what it turns into and where.

What it turns into I wonder — mamma oh la la mamma I wonder what it turns into oh I wonder into what into what.

How does it turn into what you catch or those you catch and then those you create and if you create them then with what mamma with what.

Sometimes I wonder if those you catch come from your brother's brother's father's sister's husband's brother's father's brother's mother's sister's brother's father's father. Ok so that's where they come from but how and what do they turn into what.

But maybe also out of a brother's father's brother's mother's sister we create but what and what does it turn into oh la la.

And then maybe too in a certain way what we create is a brother's father's brother his brother his brother his mother's sister his brother's father's father the husband of his father's sister maybe we create them but how out of what.

I wonder if everything has to go somewhere and if so if the words that don't leave the mouth go somewhere and where and what they do and what they turn into.

The words that don't leave the mouth called the remains go somewhere do they pile up somewhere little piles how I don't know and I wonder where.

And if they make little piles somewhere the remains and where I wonder do we have to recycle the remains to stop them from piling up.

It's all right when the words leave the mouth it's just fine but sometimes while they're leaving to say something in some part of the body a contrary thought resists.

For example I can say I fume with impatience before the *Mmm* while in another place no I'm afraid of the *Mmm* I'm afraid of the *Mmm* resists and wins.

What part of the body does I fume with impatience come from while in another part the contrary thought resists and who wins and can I fume with impatience bring talala down on my head.

When I'm afraid of the *Mmm* when in another part of the body the thought contrary to I fume with impatience before the *Mmm* resists I try to bring talala down on someone else for example x and x has to be fake.

I look for fake x who's supposed to do it and while I try to lower my lines of defense one after the other against I fume with impatience x does it for me catches or creates talala then x fades into the dark very small.

I find x to whom everything bad happens instead of to me — everything bad everything bad while to me nothing happens I take advantage of x one more time the last really the last then I let her fade into the dark very small.

This system allows me to experience inside my mind events that happen outside to substitute x for myself as an object of pity to fear for x to tremble for x who fades into the dark while nothing at all happens to me.

And none of that matters really to take already existing but fake x and make it so that everything bad happens to her in such a way that nothing happens to me is an inoperative intention since x is a fake.

Since x is a fake it can it can be done it can it can it can.

I wonder which is my favorite fake x to whom everything happens instead of to me. I've got a lot of fake xs to whom everything happens instead of to me — for example Rachel in Blade Runner is a fake x to whom all sorts of very trying things happen while to me nothing.

In Blade Runner Rachel answers the questions in the Voight-Kampf test with things like I'd take him to the doctor and I should be enough for him.

But she failed it in the end because she couldn't tell the difference between what she catches and what she creates and what that turns into and where.

If I'd take him to the doctor comes from her or from the other guy's niece — or from the other guy's niece's implants Rachel doesn't know and how it changes she doesn't know.

Rachel tries to cast her intelligence farther and farther out to discover where I'd take him to the doctor comes from but this obsessive flight exhausts her because her thoughts must do it all physically and all alone.

In Blade Runner Rachel is pursued by Blade Runner whose job is to destroy her because she's fake and he thinks that I'd take him to the doctor doesn't come from her but from Tyrell's niece's implants.

But Blade Runner whose job is of course to destroy her of course falls in love with Rachel who is his prey.

Rachel also of course falls in love with Blade Runner but the words to tell him so won't leave her mouth because she doesn't know if the words to tell him so come from her or from the other guy's niece and how that changes.

So Blade Runner in order to make the words whose source she doesn't know come out of her mouth is forced to rough her up a little to push her into the venetian blinds with a certain violence — to make her repeat:

Touch me   touch me   —   kiss me
kiss me

so that under this pressure — growing pressure
— she manages to accurately distribute her
various sensations between herself and the
other's niece's implants.

Touch me   touch me   —   kiss me
kiss me   — I want you I want you — again —
take me in your arms.

Sometimes I wonder if Rachel's looking at me when she says I'd take him to the doctor or I should be enough for him if she's looking at me from how far away mamma.

Sometimes I wonder if Rachel's looking at me when she says I'd take him to the doctor and if she's looking at me from how far away.

we kiss in america

*I believe I'm a creature a creation an invented person
I frighten small animals I vanish I blend into the
landscape — I'm a creation slightly parallel to the
one I cannot not believe that I believe in.*

My sister in two parts lives in a world in two parts one of which includes this legend. It seems that once there was a village full of beings that, under the influence of others, all at once faltered and fell to their knees and into error.

And when King John arrived to eradicate evil the worst among them went to hide in the mountain and little by little they became so mean that they changed into Cat People and did horrible things.

It's said that even today their daughters or the daughters of their daughters sometimes revert to their wildness and that they do this when their instincts are aroused.

My sister in two parts knows the story well and sometimes bits come back to her in the form of particularly frightening beings that drag her back — back to the they of they changed and she can't go further back.

And without knowing where she gets this ability to make them appear she can tell that they're drawing her very close to her sister — right to the spot where she fuses with her sister of the animal sort

So close that she then wonders which — herself true living sister or her fake Cat People sister is the more fake of the two. Her name is Irena she is my sister in two parts.

Mr. Reed who is American despite all the patience within him would very much like to kiss her because at this point in the story we kiss in America but clearly this scares her.

One part of Irena knows — she too of course that we kiss in America but her other part refuses — and there's nothing she can do without pitting his belief against her own

They changed versus we kiss in America and she has to do it because we kiss in America happens too close to the home of they changed — that's why you always have to be so careful. I had to. I had to don't you get it I had to.

When we kiss in America gets too close to they
changed only sleep calms her — which she sings
while ostensibly doing other things to watch
him sleep to watch peacefully through the win-
dow.

And when she sings sleep her voice is like a very
slight breeze or a stream of gas — so soft that
you can't tell if sleep addresses Mr. Reed or the
they of they changed

Or if it serves to soothe the two parts of Cat
People — this part and that other almost equally
intense — that which knows that we kiss in
America and that which forbids it.

And while Irena sings sleep in its lala form as long as it's not another — no please — Mr Reed, addressed by sleep to remove the they of they changed from her mind, waits, watching over her and enfolding her in his arms calls her

My little scatterbrain

Accepting that she still needs because she believes to stay within her limits to avoid becoming unhappy for the first time. Sleep for Mr. Reed sleep for they changed and don't wake up the silencer sleeping inside.

In Cat People neither Mr. Reed nor Cat People agree to become unhappy for the first time and neither stops short of doing everything possible to postpone the moment of becoming unhappy for the first time.

Him he's never been unhappy never been unhappy understood as until he got here the first time seems surprised to suddenly find himself so.

Her she refuses absolutely sensing perfectly well that to become unhappy for the first time changes — which turns out to be right and risks making her form become I had to I had to don't you get it I had to.

Her I had to form her at least I believe I hope —
in short I think — her form her I was sure of it
form — hoo hoo — I was sure of it plus the fact
that I believed

In Cat People neither Mr. Reed nor Cat People
agree to become unhappy for the first time but
that doesn't make any difference because in
spite of their determination not to do so

Because in spite of their huge determination not
to do so they're going to have to anyway both
for the first time.

I wonder what the difference is between a story and believing it — I don't understand the believing it — Dr. Judd the stories if they haven't been written down we can forget them right.

Do they get erased — each one ceding its place to a more lively one or do they accumulate — stacked up in the body — they changed versus became versus hidden in the mountain and in that case must we believe them all and how many can you contain.

Dr. Judd in the story of King John is it possible to switch off the they of they changed to erase the fact of believing it.

To say no it's nothing it's not the same nothing's happening it's nothing just very similar just to have believed to have heard it said it's nothing it's not the same nothing's going on.

No it's nothing it's not the same nothing's happening it's nothing just very similar just to have believed to have heard it said it's nothing it's not the same nothing's happening.

No it's nothing it's not the same nothing's going on it's nothing just very similar just to have believed to have heard it said it's nothing it's not the same nothing's happening. Dr. Judd said so.

My sister in two parts lives in a world whose two parts split her in two. And to save a little time it's a belief — and to make it possible to bring them together again

Given that given that it's possible to make this get lost so close to her sister and we kiss in America live together she knows she can't stop putting it off

To keep putting off the first time and yes Mr. Reed nonetheless accepts losing her in advance — because she doesn't want her two parts to die because she doesn't want it to end.

ask me a difficult question

I wonder when you take on someone else's symptom if the other loses the symptom or if the other keeps the symptom anyway and in that case if the symptom gets doubled why. Why the symptom gets doubled if apart from it we decide — between us to divide it or trade it or lend it or confide it or give it or borrow it or steal it or it it.

If I take his symptom say a wracking cough will
he keep his wracking cough anyway or will his
wracking cough leave him or will it become a lit-
tle less wracking for him. And if the cough isn't
less wracking for him if the symptom gets
doubled is it worth taking on the other's
symptom — is it worth the trouble if the cough
isn't any less wracking for him.

I wonder why hearing from our own mouth the words of others come out is such a sound and soothing thing and if you could what words of what others according to what criteria the most —and as for criteria whose. From whom to choose the criteria to use to want to hear from his own mouth the words of others come out and be they ever so sound so soothing from whom to choose — the words that's what I'm wondering.

I often hear coming out of my own mouth words that others have said — real others — real in reality but also fake others — x already extant but fake, of which I decide according to a certain resemblance a certain quality to become a kind of copy but for real in reality. And it's a lot of fun to be able to become the copy of a kind of fake other — fake but in reality real.

From a false other already extant but fake I decide and I take back everything that comes out of her mouth I talk like her speak like her — even if later I have to redistribute the feelings and gestures I attribute to myself all all that's hers — according to what criteria of approach — all the while knowing perfectly well that I could stop playing her — one among others my false twin sister dizygote her.

It's because of the cyclone — where did you see a cyclone my poor girl a cyclone you've gotten so terribly frail a cyclone my poor little one — yes it's because of the cyclone it was Monsieur Arsène who told me.

It's because of the cyclone — where did you see a cyclone my poor girl a cyclone you've gotten so terribly frail a cyclone my poor little one — yes it's because of the cyclone it was Monsieur Arsène who told me.

Like her I like to repeat the same thing several times mine those that come out of the mouths of others — no not others those that come out of Monsieur Arsène's mouth. I like to see things come out from Monsieur Arsène's mouth like it's because of the cyclone then hear them come out of my own because the same things by means of this process are no longer the same at all.

They're the same but much better because while
I hear coming out of Monsieur Arsène's mouth
it's because of the cyclone what I hear is not it's
because of but it's a cyclone and a cyclone said
by Monsieur Arsène like everything he says
is something very sound and soothing to me
because I have a secret love relationship with
Monsieur Arsène — and that makes everybody
nervous.

I wonder why that makes everybody so nervous when we enjoy making words that come out of the mouths of others come out of our mouth and exactly what kind of nervousness it is. Exactly what kind of nervousness is it that I really wonder what kind — when the words that come out of our mouths soothe us with the others within them — being the others and the secret relationships.

Out of my mouth — being she — the words don't often come out in the form of speech but when they come out to say something they almost always do it several times in a row. For example when I say listen mamma mamma I've got to tell you mamma mamma mamma mamma comes out of my mouth three times in a row three times the first — pause — his wracking cough then the two others fused fused at top speed.

And the three times are very different the first comes out as a bass and the third is very shrill more shrill than the two other almost as shrill as the second A. of A.A.A. And the third is very shrill because at the third mamma I realize that his wracking cough is his wracking cough that the symptoms get doubled and are not shared so that I lose it — mamma mamma.

I wonder if you really lose it when you lose it or if it's something else and in that case if something else resembles a single thing easy to recognize or if it's shared and makes itself felt several times and simultaneously in several places and where and how to know it and how to escape it. And is it in order to escape it that after having lost it I'm going to see — also to lose the rabbits in the rabbit hunting scene.

I don't understand why in the hunting scenes where rabbits die the rabbits writhe and die often several times in a row even if you can see perfectly well that it's the same rabbit that dies. You watch the scene and the rabbit writhes and dies then it re-writhes and re-dies in exactly the same way again. You say wait a minute that's strange this rabbit that dies and re-dies — that's strange but why does he re-die.

In reality rabbits neither writhe nor die in exactly the same way twice. They writhe in their own way which is not that of another rabbit then they die period. In reality humans sometimes writhe exactly the same way twice in a row but die only once and they die it in their own way which is not the way of other humans — they writhe and they die period.

Mouchette my dizygotic twin sister who doesn't live in reality doesn't ever writhe but she dies — that she does and she's got to do it three times in order to get it done — once for the symptoms that get doubled and no aren't shared once for the cyclone and once for her secret love relationship that makes everybody so nervous. And she does it in her own way which is not that of another. She she does it three times to get it done.

you are the business

How do you do it you push open the door —
good and afterward he asks you is it you so you
answer you tell him yes it's me hello — hello it's
me and then you kiss him — you tell him about
your day no he does that and after that what
happens — what happens after that. And he
tells in real time pretty much just what's going
on and he does it very simply like you Simon
who as soon as you arrive say it's me Simon.

I wonder if it's true like the world such as it is says that one day we'll have to give something back — that we'll have to pull out all the stops if there's a moment when we'll know it — the flower scene *(stronger)* maybe — we'll tell ourselves hold on it's my turn now we've got to pull out all the stops now and if to pull out all the stops means to make something known to someone for example.

Me too like everyone I'd really like to make something known to someone or for someone to want once again to make something known to me — someone whatever happens before the flower scene *(stronger)* — me too I'd really like to pull out all the stops but how in the form of who and what to do — do what you want replies the bad guy but I don't really know what I want.

What I want I don't know but what I do know in any case is that if I go on like this waiting for someone once again to want to make something known to me — gaining ground on talala gaining ground on the flowers *(stronger)* — between the desire to pull out all the stops and my leanings — this oh go on without me as the world such as it is says until the day that I am the business I am the business.

I wonder if it's possible to pull out all the stops while at the same time keeping talala at a distance. Me I'm afraid of business and even more of talala but if I distance talala maybe then I'll completely forget to pull out all the stops. So how can I manage not to completely forget to pull out all the stops and still want talala — in other words what is the proper distance between talala and me — that's the question that consumes me.

To hold talala close enough to me to stop forgetting to pull out all the stops but not too close nonetheless to be able to do it correctly. Unless on the contrary I have to contain it within me — talala curled up inside me among others — the flower scene *(stronger)* inside me — yes among others and don't forget to keep track of it among the others and then to pull out all the stops.

I wonder if there will be someone waiting for me at the end — someone whatever happens waiting for me in any case for example Simon if I call myself Johnny my simple-minded dizygotic young brother — and who will want to be known and be known from a flower scene *(stronger)* his and as for mine then — curled up inside me among others — and who absolutely must make something known to me.

He will have come in order to chase me all the
way back from the flower scene *(stronger)* where
it all started — will have let me pass him on
purpose he who ran ahead — he gaining ground
on talala faster than I then will have caught up
and passed me so that he can wait for me at the
end. He'll say hello — just simply hello it's me
Simon hello my boy how are you my boy.

He'll say my boy my boy how strange — will ask questions oh have you been here awhile what do you mean did you do it or not — I won't know I forgot. He'll tell me come along let's take a little walk — if you want walking's not hard will teach me other words tell me what you think then from then on look you have an extra turn — he will make the rules instead of the bad guy.

He'll want it. He'll want it because as he so well put it everyone needs to make something known to someone to give something back. And he'll want to do it now and give it back to me because he's been looking for me all this time. And will give it back to me would mean — in the form of my boy to have me and for that to take me back from the bad guy go you've got to go — to be his now.

Simon isn't all that afraid of talala but old age is there before him and the bad guy made him sad by stealing the only person that he once again wanted to make something known to. That's why he had to let everything go to learn to see another father take — a photo no photo — to leave to take to the road and follow us me and the bad guy. That's why he had to because he had to kill the one who'd made him sad.

But the one who'd made him sad once dead what to do — for what to do with someone who's made us sad once he's dead. Simon's not all that afraid of talala but he needs another in its place — to whom once again to make something known — still before the flower scene *(stronger)* — to know what happens later. He needs it. He needs it. And because he needs it I don't mind no since in any case I don't mind doing it.

So no matter what he wants to make known to me for him I'll agree to serve as the other to Simon Hirsch — even a spare — the extra turn as he says that he'll call my boy my boy how not the boys to pull out all the stops and be everything to him — how do you do it you push open the door — of everything whatever happens — no matter as long as he looks for me finds me wants me to pull out all the stops for him.

I'm telling you just like that you who are neither
family nor family Simon I really want I mean I'd
really like   no matter what to give you my
flower scene *(stronger)* inside me among others
to give you something back — and to do it in the
form of a boy if I have to Johnny if I have to my
boy my simple-minded dizygotic brother — and
I do it very willingly very simply like you Simon
because I am the business.

Then once it's done — I can sleep next to you —
of course if you'd like my boy Simon will reply
moving over to make room. And so I am happy.

touch there touch

My name is Patty Duke. Patty Duke as Helen.
That's new for me and suddenly I wonder if it's
really possible to have two first names and why
as Helen I feel so Patty. Yes but Anne is so Anne
and Patty so Helen. And if Patty is so Helen
there's nothing surprising in the fact that me too
I can be so Patty.

As Patty I have hands in place of eyes and ears a mouth but it can't talk a head with no memory — and the things that come to me are always already there so close that I can touch them and then they're gone just like that with no warning.

And I can't let myself start to love them because they go away so far when they go away without my being able to tell when they'll go away or know if they'll come back or if gone maybe — and forever it seems unless I go away with them.

And I don't know whether I miss them or whether I erase even the memory of them to keep from being carried away with them — so that they leave me in peace with mamma which is to say the whole world because for me the whole world has the shape of mamma.

And if for me the whole world takes on the shape of mamma and if touch is like sight — when she holds me in her hands her arms her mamma dress I find myself under the watch of the whole world.

But if for me the whole world takes on the shape of mamma when mamma leaves — mamma which is to say all mamma all her it's the whole world that goes away with her as if being seen is gone who knows — and forever.

And what do you do in a head with no memory so that mamma left doesn't necessarily mean all mamma all her — *Mmm* the world and me in its wake all gone me too who knows — and forever. So sometimes because of the whole world I cry when I touch mamma's mouth.

When I cry when I touch mamma's mouth I
don't know if I cry in fact I mean like cry like
mamma or is it something else — *Mmm* all but a
cry. But what's there in — *Mmm* all but a cry is
all that's strange throughout the whole world
that I don't understand.

I don't understand why things when they've
gone leave nothing behind — nor why to leave
me in peace with mamma they force me like that
to get them out of my head why — and forever.

I still don't understand and sometimes it makes
me panic to the point that a kind of rage overtakes
me — *Mmm* causing a strong I want for which
I'd like to construct a form inside then push it
out hoping it will go somewhere and be caught.

But as nothing of me sees nothing that leaves how can I tell what I want is like and if I want works — how can I determine I want's effective range unless it comes back increased by something else.

And in when it comes back when always too long is the hardest part — because in order for me to be calm I want must leave and work and signal and come back increased by something else — and all this right away without when because I'm afraid of when.

Because for as long as when lasts I want lasts if it's late coming back increased by something else it's everything but then everything — all mamma all she and me in her wake — *Mmm* the whole world which goes away all at once who knows — and forever. So sometimes because of the whole world I cry when I touch mamma's mouth.

Mmm is said with back of the hand on cheek mamma's
missing is said when mamma when mamma's missing
me missing too.

Is said with arms held out in front so that it will come back
that I want that I have no more something else
will be returned to me.

Is said with the fingers on mamma's mouth too large
too long too fear all too when time
drags that when lasts.

One day with big hand inside of hand that falls — *Mmm* someone touches with big hand inside of hand that seeks — *Mmm* someone gives then thing there in hand touch then thing there touch there touch then thing there for you touch then thing

That I touch in fact but as she traces a legible t of touch in hand the thing disappears. One day in the form of a big hand at the end of which a being is attached though I don't know why I think so war on me is declared.

I know that it's war because from this being at the end of the big hand and that I call violent person — complete opposite of mamma I can tell she won't give in if it's not against something else.

I don't want to have to but the hand attached at the end to the violent person and which is imposed upon me to use as if it were my own decides otherwise falls upon me with force — pressing into my hand things that I in fact touch.

And while finally I manage to bend myself to its will which is to say to do what the hand does without understanding at first and without really knowing what I'm feeling while it's waiting for something more from me much more.

And what it puts into much more is what's between thing that I touch touch and touch I find — *Mmm* this thing I don't know but that they call words. And I am sure that it won't let go the whole time it takes to get it into my head that these words mean things.

That words mean things I still don't know at all
and since my ears refuse to hear the being at the
end of the big hand to make me understand
after each touch there touch makes it move
inside my own.

And the hand says yes Helen there is a word for
that that has a word this means a word and the
word means this thing — there's a word that
means that. Yes the chicks hatch from their eggs
things come to you — no they aren't miraculous
accidents they come and go.

No you don't have to go with them let them
come back — yes things that have gone can
come back in your mind that's what words do.
Yes the luminous track left by words means that
the things — you'll see can be kept in your
mind.

And again and again — me with the word the
word with the thing me with the thing still —
reciprocal relations around the same objects in
such a way that one day at the end of a million
words perhaps between thing that I touch touch
and touch — its word I don't know, making a
bridge.

So while the places that another's eyes see for
me form the frame I try in the nice bad way that
only I know to imagine how far away the objects
people animals others are that the big hand
refers to and the categories to which they belong.

Nice bad sharp smell nice chick hatching from
its egg nice water bad stone bad fence nice bird
bad Anne nice mamma bad Helen. Bad.

And so from strategy to strategy and as far away as possible from mamma in whose wake the air is too sweet Anne constructs her war in which the enemy is a little girl — a tyrant who can't see hears nothing and constructs it with discipline as her primary weapon and victory as her single goal.

Which means making me surpass my limits putting her you within my limits her you inside I inside *Mmm* — even in the air I breathe — making *Mmm* grow inside me changing its shape.

Then another thing called defer — yes to when and that's why words because violent person knows perfectly well that if word means thing then it's possible that when will cease to be forever and that in fact thing will come back. And if thing comes back in fact then yes let it go.

I don't understand the idea that I had to forget everything for example that once I knew how to say WoWo but couldn't retain it — only mamma knows

That I had to become inept again all at once struck by an inertia that pulled me back — and then make a detour passing through Patty — so much Patty so much Helen — through touch there touch — yes to when so that things in fact come back.

I don't understand why I have to defer to another — to the war — why to Anne exactly while Anne isn't mamma while Anne — violent person is the complete opposite of mamma.

If everything is big if everything is different if *Mmm* takes variable forms in turn — if mamma world she and me in her wake — and forever is not the whole world it could be there that I lose — Teacher

Because I'm afraid if mamma for mamma that much air makes distant — if mamma for mamma that mamma world all mamma all she will no longer be the whole world and if that's so what to do in the whole world's arms if it's really huge.

Unless it switches—if mamma for mamma my arms it might be possible for her to fit in them and I in hers who knows to be the world for her one day — me the world like her — we both in the whole world watching over — who over whom.

Simone Simon

When I say I'm named Simone Simon I wonder
if it's because I dream a form almost perfect
open odd even quasi-identic the hidden silent

hidden in the closed fold nothing that overflows
though e jars the ensemble a little it glitches it's
the play in the system that thwarts the symmetric.

Or if my Simon stutters indecisive like I needed
two this first name plus this first name almost
equally intense if it's not the silent plus

plus the emptiness my Simon stutters in place a
decisive name which both exceeds and repeats
the excess in its mute form and repeats it to force
it to hold.

Or Simon name of daddy so slightly exceeded
because I'm a girl inscribed inside with the
silent and so that I *Mmm* there name of daddy
in my own

in my own like *Mmm* so that I *Mmm* there how
not how while my Simon name of daddy while
my name my name of daddy beats on.

Or if for want of my e no not really not know-
ing what it is nor where nor how to know it by
sight nor similarity nor what it holds inside nor
nor

nor secret nor known to me alone for want of my
e not e my indeterminate zone or else my zone
there where nothing looks like nothing else
which is not such a bad place to live.

Or if after looks so much like before the same
trait for trait it's barely there all over again the
same super-known that why did it want my e
why if it's true

if it's true like it seems that after so much before
and if it's for the same once again the same
already by heart exhausting at the end so why
want it why.

For whom for one so mine after my favorite so
more mine of my favorite so mine so why is it
needed so badly and why be surprised that it
sticks

that my e sticks my so mine so before that it
wavers looks once twice for because of it of my
so mine before my favorite so mine.

Or if I accepted me hidden in my e the sight the voice of Simon to the point that I contain them to the point that they twist me into Simon girl-version

and e like a girl-version addition the emptiness and the solid earth of the other side in its boy form its form again the again of my end of the earth straight ahead.

Or if my e my convergence the spot where my
Simons converse my favorites they on whom I
rest and at least I can shelter their corner and
make them

make them talk to each other answer right in
the middle of the e in the middle of which I'm
finally silenced I listen hold thrive me simply
crossed in this e of encounter.

Or if me framed by why two my Simon its alter
why the second another or its understudy its
replay or extension I go

even so a little further I go and if two looks that
much like it I think it's that I'll need to recognize
it by the sound in order to want it the two.

By the sound to settle on to invent something
like a ménage à trois even if two gangs up
against three in order to escape so that there
remains at worst

at worst at least a pas de deux as nothing more
than two for if you picture it and how while it
remains at worst to avoid its remaining at most.

Or if trying to frighten me to not be which is to
say without gender in short nothing known
nothing that plays a part but changes just as well
to an animal as to a stone as to a

thing as to a stone a something anything what-
ever it takes as long as it can what a relief refuse
to change face could keep its neutral form.

Or if my silent e frozen sea there I'm scared between two like two poles two sides of sea frozen straight through frozen e that it might shatter there that it might break

two axes anything to break frozen sea times two for we're not too two against that frozen sea two weapons two axes to break to wreck the frozen sea.

When I say I'm named Simone Simon I don't
know if it's for the thrill of not deciding it
swings between two times the same but for the
e that makes what difference

e what or fear of this space on the edge or to be
escorted not by me alone I don't want me alone
always escorted but by what so all right that.

You be the Argentine and I'll be Chéri Bibi that's
how it starts. You be the Argentine because it's
got to be you who clears away the chairs for me
at the end and me Chéri Bibi alias Chouquina
alias Sweet Potato or Merryl Lazy Moon —
whatever try it try seeing a character bearing
whatever name whose only action will be to
do nothing — just be there sleeping wedged
in between my cast-off memories my smiling
future and you'll be watching over me my Tall
Argentine.

That's how it starts — a story with lots of characters neither good nor bad where everyone does what he can which is to say any which way step by step. Some walk not seeing others watch cry others clear away the chairs and I don't know if it's better to clear away the chairs or to walk between the cleared away chairs others pass batons accidents memories accidents and I there inside like on stand-by and hopeless I must be asleep.

And there I am inside like gone without having done a thing for while the days stream on thanks to what accrues I translate the echoes of the outside world as a flood of silent associations — Chéri Bibi is in a coma Cheri Bibi gets ready for later. And because it's a matter of that having seen nothing coming and not having expected what's happening Chéri Bibi seems hard to beat at her game because from there — Chéri Bibi barely a body and without endings what more can you do if not nothing and then come back.

That's just where I didn't want to go no stop a moment — take my motionless position of a being in a place that's not a place to live but where you could bear whatever name any old clothes that tie up on both sides and the body does nothing but the head you can picture it hoarding — listen Chouquina then come back all the chairs cleared away so that I neither bump against nor fall upon and set up for a new start. That's what I wanted yes but now who's going to clear away the chairs.

Simply by imagining the number of massages and treatments and changes of linen and fingernails and haircuts, solicitous gestures — they work at it together and their hands work in concert to untie my knots he tells me stories of chairs cleared away because he believes in miracles that he loves me and that he wants me to come back — that's how the batons go. And those two he who's talking to me she who's rocking me what do you call it when they're not called parents.

You be the Argentine, ok — because it's got to be you who waits for me tells me when to come back and what to do with you because I won't even know whether I would have had to leave just long enough for the others to have already left for a whole new future and without conflict or on the contrary if I would want even with you both of them to have added a one to make the number uneven — and if therefore the want is greater to be the one than one of the two. You'd know wouldn't you.

Hoping that you'd know this me I'm there calm and I do whatever I want in my head. And if I do whatever I want in my head I can decide to look like him or her — one or the other without distinction or one with its distinctions which really isn't so bad — for example Chéri Bibi was a dancer Chéri Bibi is in a coma but I don't have to choose — Chéri Bibi plus Chéri Bibi danced complex pose in coma oblique and should I ever manage to strike these two poses I think I could truly become her.

And if I do whatever I want in my head so I could draw you for example — I can say you will be the Argentine me Chéri Bibi or the opposite you really want to be my Tall Argentine sure why not or the opposite — or I'm the Cuban or the opposite and if I become the Cuban a way like any other to give an old wrong answer to a question asked American-style though I really can become most great person possible — then you I could love you and start to love others too.

I wonder where I got this idea that to be most great person possible is a matter of the number of returns — of turns if turns there are — the notion that you've got to leave and why as an accident as if you had to have disappeared purely and simply by surprise and without explanation then shot again straight up to the peak without going through the steps to earn that position — if turn there is all chairs cleared away a greatest person possible.

Is it because the motion gives me the feeling of a sinuous curve that I avoid heights for fear of descents — or to pretend I'm disappearing, setting the stage for my shocking and glorious return after my praises have been sung — don't cry lovely dove it must be said — or the pleasure of beginnings of beginnings of another first time or for — hidden between two perspectives which is to say protected awaiting the perfect moment — because of this fixed idea that any place always already inscribed becomes its opposite.

I wonder where I got this mania for accidents but if turn there is in any case and even if the turn of all chairs cleared away lasts almost as long as don't cry my dove from where will it come — from what better place within what's moving if not so on this side so this side and late — and what to do between each if not nothing then come back. Late like high voltage like having already walked out or something like that or even less — anything then make it as different as possible then get a running start burst out all at once.

You be the Argentine me Chéri Bibi it's like that this time. You will have waited patiently for my return — why me with no reason all valid but not holding and I'd really like I think the whys run out just like the one after another because we're here in this world where everyone does what he can which is to say any which way step by step — I think I'd really like to. And since I'd really like to and since I do what I want in my mind and anyway why not.

Note

Caroline Dubois lives in Paris and teaches at the Ecole des Beaux-Arts in Rueil-Malmaison. She has translated American poets like Norma Cole and Deborah Richards. *c'est toi le business* is her most recent book (2005). Earlier books include *je veux être physique* [I want to be physical] of 1999, *Arrête maintenant* [Stop now] of 2001 and *Malécot* (2003). "Stop Now" has been published in English in *Verse* 24, Nos. 1-3 (2007), also translated by Cole Swensen.

Cole Swensen's books of poetry include *The Book of a Hundred Hands, The Glass Age, Noon, Try,* and *Such Rich Hour.* She has translated Pierre Alferi, Olivier Cadiot, Pascalle Monnier, Jean Frémon and others. Both her poetry and her translations have won many prizes.